History and activities of the
Roman Empire

Alexandra Fix

Heinemann

www.heinemann.co.uk/library
Visit our website to find out more information about Heinemann Library books.

To order:
☎ Phone 44 (0) 1865 888066
 Send a fax to 44 (0) 1865 314091
📄 Visit the Heinemann Bookshop at www.heinemann.co.uk/library to browse our
💻 catalogue and order online.

First published in Great Britain by Heinemann Library, Halley Court, Jordan Hill, Oxford OX2 8EJ, part of Harcourt Education. Heinemann is a registered trademark of Harcourt Education Ltd.

Editorial: Audrey Stokes
Design: Kimberly R. Miracle in collaboration with Cavedweller Studio
Picture research: Mica Brancic
Production: Vicki Fitzgerald

Origination: Chroma Graphics
Printed and bound in China by WKT Company Limited

13-digit ISBN 978 0431080871 (hardback)
11 10 09 08 07
10 9 8 7 6 5 4 3 2 1

13-digit ISBN 978 0431080956 (paperback)
12 11 10 09 08
10 9 8 7 6 5 4 3 2 1

British Library Cataloguing in Publication Data
Fix, Alexandra, 1950-
Roman Empire. – (Hands on ancient history)
1. Rome – Civilization – Juvenile literature
2. Rome – History – Juvenile literature
I. Title
937
A full catalogue record for this book is available from the British Library.

Acknowledgements
The author and publishers are grateful to the following for permission to reproduce photographs: Ancient Art and Architecture Collection, p. **11**; Bridgeman Art Library, pp. **10** (Private Collection), **12** (Museo della Civilta Romana, Rome, Italy, Giraudon), **18** (Ephesus Museum, Turkey); Corbis, pp. **4** (Bob Krist), **7** (Richard T. Nowitz), **8** (Archivo Iconografico, S.A.), **9** (Vanni Archive), **13** (Nathan Benn), **14** (Araldo de Luca), **15** (Alinari Archives), **16** (Richard T. Nowitz), **22** (Gianni Dagli Orti); Getty Images, p. **26** (National Geographic).

Cover photographs of a Roman mosaic (foreground) reproduced with permission of Corbis/Araldo de Luca and the Colosseum (background) reproduced with permission of Getty Images/Photodisc.

The publishers would like to thank Greg Aldrete, Eric Utech and Kathy Peltan for their assistance in the preparation of this book.

Contents

Chapter 1: Rise and fall of the Roman Empire 4

Chapter 2: Roman communities and families 10

Chapter 3: Roman fun. 14

Chapter 4: Hands-on ancient history. 16

    Recipe: *libum* (sacrificial cake) 16

    Activity: make a horizontal sundial 18

    Activity: create a mosaic 22

    Activity: Roman dice games 26

Glossary 30

More books to read 30

A note to teachers 31

Index. 32

Some words are shown in bold, **like this.** You can find out what they mean by looking in the glossary.

Chapter 1: Rise and fall of the Roman Empire

Rome was founded around 753 BCE. It was built on seven hills above the Tiber River in Italy. One thousand years later, it was the centre of the largest, most powerful empire in the ancient world. The Romans' inventions and ideas still affect our lives today.

According to a Roman story, the god of war had twin sons. They were named Romulus and Remus, and they were raised by a female wolf. When they grew up, Romulus became leader of Rome. A man named Romulus really did become Rome's first king. Kings began to rule Rome in 753 BCE. Each king passed the rule on to his chosen follower.

By 509 BCE many Romans were unhappy with the kings. They wanted to choose their ruler, so they formed a **republic**. Now, instead of a king, there was a senate. Roman **citizens** voted for the senators. Each year two men were elected as consuls. They led the senate.

About dates

The phrases BC and BCE show that something happened before Jesus was born. The phrases CE and AD show that something happened after Jesus was born. On this timeline you can see that Rome was founded 753 years before Jesus was born. The empire ended 476 years after Jesus's birth. With modern dates we do not usually use CE or AD. Everyone assumes we are talking about today.

Timeline

753 BCE
Rome is founded

753–509 BCE
Rome is a monarchy

509–27 BCE
Rome is a republic

A portion of the Roman Colosseum still stands today. This huge stadium was once home to the famous gladiator fights.

59 BCE
Julius Caesar is elected consul

44 BCE
Julius Caesar is killed

27 BCE–14 CE
Augustus Caesar rules

307 CE
Constantine becomes emperor

27 BCE–476 CE
Rome is an empire

476 CE
Roman Empire is defeated

Constant fighting for power in the senate eventually weakened the **republic**. Julius Caesar, one of its last elected consuls, was killed by enemies in 44 BCE. His murder drove the empire into disorder. In 27 BCE, Octavian became emperor. He was the adopted great-nephew of Julius Caesar. He was given the new name Augustus by the senate. He restored order and brought peace. From this point on the emperor was the sole ruler of the whole Roman Empire. This was very different from the way the consuls had ruled.

The empire expands

The Roman army was well organized and very successful. They kept enlarging the empire by defeating other countries. Each captured area became a Roman **province**. Walls and forts kept enemies out of these provinces. Sometimes, people felt safer after they were conquered by the Romans. Towns grew up around the army camps.

New goods and ideas

Soldiers brought new goods and ideas from the provinces back to Rome. Unusual foods, beautiful jewels, and strange animals were imported. Ideas about art, architecture, literature, and religion were also brought to Rome. Romans worshipped many gods. When they conquered a country, they often added the gods of that country to their own.

 All Romans paid taxes to support the army and to give tribute to the emperor.

By 117 BCE, Rome controlled all of the countries surrounding the Mediterranean Sea.

The end of the empire

The Roman Empire lasted for about 500 years. Augustus was followed by more than 60 emperors. Among the most famous were Tiberius, Caligula, Claudius, Nero, Hadrian, Caracalla, Trajan, and Justinian. In 307 CE, Constantine became emperor. He was the last strong emperor. After his death, his sons fought for power. This divided and weakened the empire again. Romans began to lose control in Britain, Gaul (modern-day France), North Africa, and Spain. The final downfall came in 476 CE. A German named Odoacer removed the last Roman emperor and declared himself King of Italy.

Roman ideas we still use today

Under the Emperor Justinian, Romans recorded the principles behind their laws in a book called the Justinian Code. Those ideas still form the basis of the justice system in many countries around the world, including the United States and the United Kingdom.

Engineering ideas

The Romans were talented engineers. They built many roads between the city of Rome and its **provinces**. Roads were wide and straight so that army troops could march easily. Roman engineers designed buildings using new materials. They created concrete from a mixture of broken stones, lime, sand, volcanic ash, and water. The concrete was waterproof and especially good for bridges and **aqueducts**. Aqueducts were pipes that carried water downhill from the mountain springs miles away. Fresh water was delivered to public baths, town fountains, and some private homes. They built sewers with underground pumps and pipes, taking old water from fountains, baths, and toilets.

The arch was not new, but Romans expanded its use. Arches made it less costly to build long bridges and aqueducts.

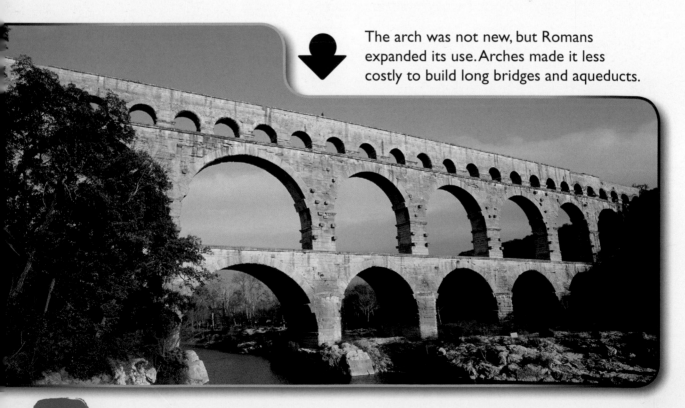

This domed building could hold an imaginary ball as tall as a 12-storey building.

Romans also built structures to celebrate their emperors, and temples to honour their gods. Using concrete and arches that crossed over each other, the Romans created the dome. The Pantheon is a temple with one of the largest concrete domes ever built. It still stands today.

One smaller engineering idea was perfecting the horizontal sundial. Sundials were used to tell time and are still used today as garden decorations.

Letters and language from Rome

The Roman alphabet used the same letters you are looking at now. It is the most widely used alphabet today. More than a quarter of all English words have their roots in Latin, the language of ancient Rome. This includes everyday words, as well as medical, scientific, and legal words. Several languages are based on Latin, including French, Spanish, Italian, Portuguese, and Romanian. These are called the Romance languages. "Romance" comes from the word Roman.

Chapter 2: Roman communities and families

Cities were the centre of Roman life. One million people lived in the city of Rome. Most people lived in apartment buildings up to six storeys high. Ordinary families might have a single room. Middle-class families would have several rooms. Apartments were small so people spent a lot of the day outdoors. People walked everywhere, and the narrow streets were crowded. Wheeled vehicles were banned during the day. Rome was dark, busy, noisy, and dangerous at night.

 Rome was a busy city where people lived, worked, relaxed, worshipped, and governed their community.

Social classes

Most Romans were plebians, common people who worked for others. Some were craftspersons, farmers, shepherds, or fishermen.

Equites were **citizens** who owned the workshops, stores, and apartments. Women and men had jobs in workshops, hotels, and shops. Children worked with their parents to bring in extra money. Patricians were wealthy, upper-class landowners. They often owned hundreds of slaves from conquered countries. Some slaves were well educated and worked as teachers, doctors, and clerks.

Roman citizens

In the United States and the UK everyone born in the country is a citizen. Many other people can become citizens. In ancient Rome only some men were citizens. Women could never become citizens. Children were not citizens, but boys became citizens when they were 16. Male slaves could be freed or buy their freedom and then become citizens. Sometimes, all of the men of a conquered community were given citizenship. At other times, only the rich were allowed to become citizens. Men in the **provinces** could also become citizens by joining the Roman army.

 This stone relief shows a Roman butcher at work. He is cutting meat on a wooden chopping block, something still used in meat markets today.

Roman home life

The father was head of a Roman household. His wife, children, and slaves belonged to him. They had no rights of their own. Women cared for the home and family. Girls married as young as 12 years old. Boys married a little older. Most families had two or three children. Male children were preferred.

Wealthier boys and girls were able to go to school when they were aged 6. There were no public schools so parents hired a teacher. Students learned reading, writing, and arithmetic. Boys could attend school until they were 14. Girls left school earlier to learn how to run a household from their mothers.

Keeping people happy

There were more poor Romans than rich Romans. Many people did not have jobs. Emperors worried that the poor Romans would become angry. They gave Roman **citizens** a portion of grain. They also gave them free entry to chariot races. Today, we sometimes say politicians confuse people with "bread and circuses". This means they take attention away from real problems. The phrase comes from this Roman practice.

Romans enjoyed their mealtimes. Family and friends would eat and talk together about news, sports, politics, art, and literature.

Food and clothing

Romans ate a light breakfast of bread and cheese. At lunch they might add meat and fruit. The main meal was eaten in the late afternoon. This was often a simple meat or vegetable stew. It was cooked in the apartment or bought from a food stand.

Most Roman men wore a sleeveless knee-length tunic. For important occasions they would wear a toga. Women wore simple, full-length white tunics. They might also wear a coloured shawl over their tunic. Sandals were the most common footwear.

Mosaics in homes and public buildings often showed scenes from the everyday life of wealthy Romans.

Chapter 3: Roman fun

Roman children played with toys we would recognize today. They had kites, hoops, tops, blocks, and dolls. Draughts was a favourite board game that is still played today. Dice games and tossing coins were popular. One game, called knucklebones, used small animal bones as dice. Jacks were played by throwing stones up and catching them on the back of the hand. Children also played ball games.

For entertainment, many Romans enjoyed theatre, storytellers, musicians, puppeteers, acrobats, and performing animals. Romans liked watching and joining in sports such as wrestling, and track and field events.

In the centre of Rome's hills, was the Forum. This was a large, public, gathering space. In and around the Forum there were government buildings, libraries, gardens, and temples for the community. The public baths were a very popular place to meet friends, relax, exercise, or even hold business meetings.

This is a child's pull-along toy from ancient Rome.

Chariot races and gladiators

More than 100 festivals were celebrated each year. They were in honour of Roman gods and goddesses. The emperor hosted days of chariot races. The Circus Maximus was a favourite racetrack. It was a stadium that held 250,000 spctators. The crowds loved these dangerous, high-speed races, but fights often broke out among the fans.

Gladiator contests were also popular. They were held at the Colosseum. Trained fighters fought against each other. Wild beasts were brought suddenly up from cages below to face a single gladiator. Most gladiators were slaves or criminals who were forced to be gladiators. Some free men signed on, hoping to win prize money. There were even a few female gladiators.

Roman fans cheered for their favourite gladiators, just as we support popular sports players today.

By doing the hands-on activities in this chapter, you will get a feel for what life was like for people who lived and worked in the Roman Empire.

Recipe: libum (sacrificial cake)

Libum is a special Roman cake soaked with honey. It was sometimes offered as a sacrifice to the gods who protected Roman homes. A copy of this recipe exists from ancient Rome. It was found in a collection of simple recipes for farmers, written by Cato. He was one of the Roman consuls, or leaders, when Rome was a **republic**.

Ingredients and supplies
- wooden spoon
- 2 mixing bowls
- baking tray
- 125 g plain flour
- 240 g ricotta cheese
- 1 egg, beaten
- 125 ml honey

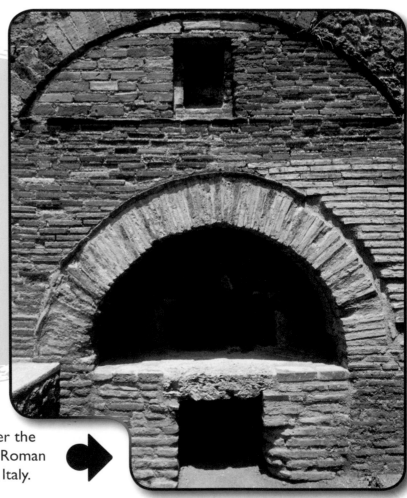

Bricks form an arch over the opening of this ancient Roman oven, found in Pompeii, Italy.

Roman *libum*

(cheese cake soaked with honey) (serves 4)

1 Preheat oven to 220° C (425° F, gas mark 7).

2 Measure flour into a bowl.

3 In another bowl, stir the cheese with a wooden spoon until it is soft.

4 Add the egg to the cheese and beat the mixture with a wooden spoon.

5 Stir the egg and cheese mixture into the flour.

6 Mix until it becomes a soft dough, and divide into 4 pieces.

7 Form each piece into a cake shape and place them on a greased baking tray.

8 Cover the cakes* and bake for 35–40 minutes, or until golden-brown.

9 Remove the cakes from the oven and cool slightly.

10 Warm the honey and pour it into a serving dish.

11 Place the warm cakes into the honey, so that they absorb the honey.

12 Allow the cakes to soak in the honey for 30 minutes before serving.

*The Romans often covered their food while it was cooking with a domed clay cover called a *testo*. You can use an upside-down pot, a metal bowl, a casserole dish, or a foil tent as a cover.

Roman *libum*

Wash your hands well if you plan to eat your *libum* Roman-style. The Romans did not use cutlery. Instead, they ate with their hands.

Activity: make a horizontal sundial

Sundials tell time by measuring shadows cast by the sun on markers each hour of the day. Even though the Egyptians used it first, the Romans improved the horizontal sundial. Romans also invented a portable sundial for travellers. They were also first to use sundials in their gardens.

Warning!

Read all the directions before beginning the project.

The Latin words *carpe diem* were often carved on Roman sundials. It means "seize the day". This reminds us to make good use of each day.

Supplies

- modelling clay that can be baked
- strong glue
- 1 chopstick
- ceramic plant saucer
- protractor
- pencil
- masking tape or chalk
- acrylic or other waterproof paint and brush

1 Look in an atlas to find out the latitude where you live.

2 Roll a small ball of clay and stick it on the end of the chopstick. Turn the ceramic saucer upside down, and press the clay onto the centre of the saucer. Use the protractor to angle the chopstick pointer, called a gnomon, to the same degree latitude as where you live. (See Picture A)

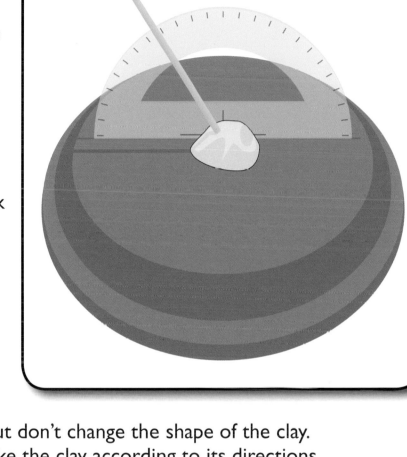

A

3 Remove the clay and the gnomon from the saucer, but don't change the shape of the clay. Ask an adult to bake the clay according to its directions. Then glue the gnomon back in place and glue the clay to the saucer.

4 Take the sundial outside and place it on a level spot. Turn the sundial so the gnomon points north. At noon, use a pencil to mark where the gnomon makes a shadow on the outer edge of the saucer.

B

5 Don't move your sundial! Every hour, make another mark where the gnomon's shadow falls on the edge of the saucer. (See Picture B)

6 Mark your sundial's original position with masking tape or chalk, so that you can put it back there later. Bring your sundial inside. Use paints to show where you marked the hours and to decorate your sundial. (See Picture C)

7 Place your sundial back in its original position. It will remain accurate until the clocks change in the spring or autumn. When the clocks move backwards or forwards, carefully rotate the entire saucer at 12:00 midday just enough to make the gnomon shadow fall on noon once again.

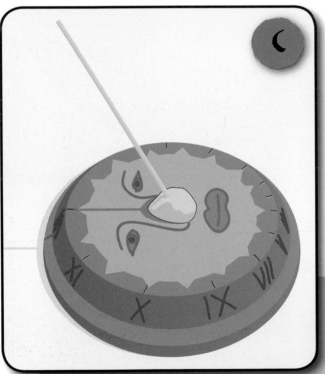

C

How would your life be different if you didn't have clocks and watches? Wouldn't it be fun to try going for one whole day without using a clock? How would you know when to eat or sleep or play?

Sundial

Sundials were one of the first types of clocks. You can keep track of time with a sundial by measuring where the shadows fall.

Where to put your sundial

There are two tricks to placing a sundial. One is to mount it outside at the correct angle to the earth. This angle is the same as the latitude where you live. You can discover your latitude by looking it up in an atlas. The other trick is to align the sundial with true north, which can vary from the magnetic north that a compass will show. True north is the direction of the North Pole in relation to where you are. To discover true north, find a level spot where you will place your sundial when you have finished making it. Place a pole or stick upright in the ground on this spot. On a sunny day, use small sticks or some stones to mark the end of the pole's shadow every 15 minutes throughout the middle part of the day. Notice where the shadow is the shortest, and stretch a string or rope from the bottom of the pole to this mark. This line from the pole to your mark, points directly to the north. Mark this direction and make a note of it so you will know where to place your sundial later.

This ancient Roman mosaic shows a man leading a strong horse into an amphitheatre for a chariot race.

Warning!

Make sure you read all the directions before beginning the project.

Activity: create a mosaic

Wealthy Romans decorated their floors and walls with mosaics. Mosaics were created with small pieces of tile, stone, or glass placed into plaster. When looked at from a distance, the coloured pieces made a picture. Some mosaics were very strong and lasted for hundreds of years. One reason we know so much about the ancient Roman city of Pompeii is that mosaics survived under the volcanic ash that buried the city. When archaeologists discovered the mosaics, they saw pictures of what life was like almost 2,000 years ago.

Supplies
- drawing paper and a pencil
- assorted colours of paper or felt, cut into small pieces (if you prefer, you can buy actual mosaic pieces at a craft shop)
- scissors
- glue
- ruler
- cardboard (optional)

1 Line the edge of your ruler up with one edge of the paper, so that you can draw along the other edge of the ruler. Do this on all four sides of your paper so you have a frame around the edge. (See Picture A)

2 Decorate the frame by drawing a pattern. (See Picture B)

3 Draw a picture of people, animals, a natural environment, buildings, or your own idea, inside the frame.

4 Optional step: glue your drawing to a piece of cardboard.

5 Carefully glue the pieces of coloured paper or felt to your drawing so that you fill in spaces one at a time. Use colours that make sense so that other people will understand your picture. Don't forget to fill the frame pattern with colours as well. (See Picture C)

Hints:
You can fill curved spaces by angling the pieces as you place them side by side.

You can make your mosaic look even more authentic if you leave a small space between each piece of paper or felt.

Mosaic

Use your finished mosaic to decorate a wall in your home. Roman mosaics often filled an entire wall.

What scene did you draw? What scene would a Roman child draw? What differences might there be between them? Have you included anything that a Roman child might never have seen? What might surprise you about the Roman child's drawing?

Activity: Roman dice games

Roman children enjoyed playing games with dice. It was fun to see who would be lucky enough to roll the highest score.

Supplies
- thick paper or brown envelopes
- pencil
- different-coloured pencil or marker pen
- ruler
- scissors
- glue or tape

Warning!
Read all directions before beginning the project.

This Roman gameboard is made of wood. The dice are made from bones and the game pieces are a stone known as amber.

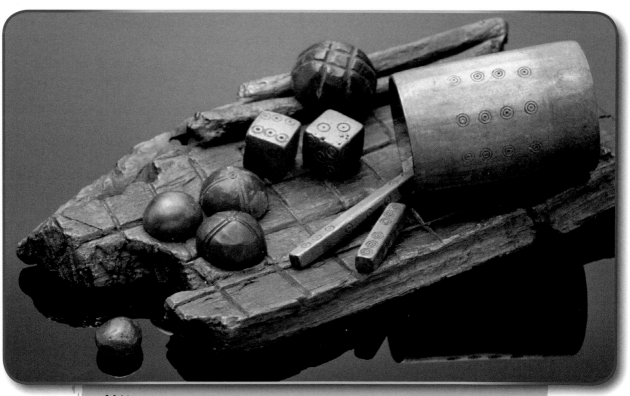

What are some of your favourite board games? How does playing a board game differ from playing computer and video games?

1 Copy the pattern of the hexamine below on to the thick paper. If you want, you can make a photocopy of the pattern, cut it out and tape it to the thick paper. You may want to enlarge the photocopy before cutting it out. (See Picture A)

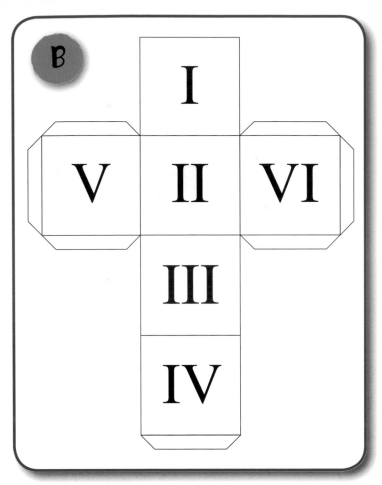

B

I

V   II   VI

III

IV

❷ Write the Roman numerals 1–6 (I, II, III, IV, V, VI) on the squares of the pattern. (See Picture B)

❸ The rectangle shapes at the ends of the pattern are your tabs for holding the die together.

❹ Carefully cut the hexamine out of the thick paper. Fold along the lines of the squares so that you create a six-sided die. Glue the tabs down to hold the die together. (See Picture C)

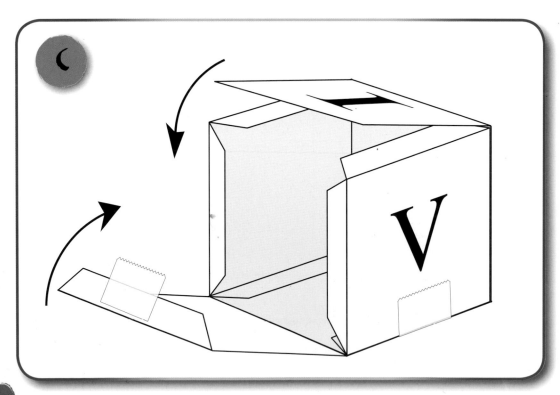

C

V

How to play "pig"

This game is similar to games played in ancient Rome.

Goal: the first player to get a total of 100 points wins.
Number of players: 2 or more
Supplies: paper for keeping score, six-sided die.

- On his or her turn, a player continues to roll the die and add up the points of each roll.
- A player's turn continues until either:
  - a one is rolled, or
  - the player chooses to hold and stop rolling.
- If a one is rolled, the player's turn ends and no points are earned.
- If the player chooses to hold (stop rolling), all of the points rolled during that turn are added to his or her score. Play continues until one player reaches 100.

How do you decide when to keep rolling and when to hold?

Dice

When you roll a pair of ones with dice, people call this "snake eyes". Does a pair of Roman numeral ones look more, or less, like snake eyes to you?

Glossary

aqueduct structure for carrying water

citizen person who is a member of a country and has certain rights and duties to that country

province parts of a country that are away from the main area

republic form of government in ancient Rome with senators elected by the citizens

More books to read

Craft Topics: The Romans, Nicola Baxter and Rachel Wright (Watts Publishing, 2001)

Excavating the Past: Ancient Rome, Fiona Macdonald (Heinemann Library, 2004)

Find Out About: Ancient Rome, Jane Bingham (Hodder & Stoughton Childrens, 2006)

Gods and Goddesses: In the Daily Life of the Ancient Romans, Peter Hicks (Hodder & Stoughton Childrens, 2003)

History Opens Windows: The Ancient Romans, Jane Shuter (Heinemann Library, 2006)

Understanding People in the Past: The Ancient Romans, Rosemary Rees (Heinemann Library, 2006)

The instructions for the crafts and activities are designed to allow pupils to work as independently as possible. However, it is always a good idea to make a prototype before assigning any project so that pupils can see how their own work will look when completed. Prior to introducing these activities, teachers should collect and prepare the materials and be ready for any modifications that may be necessary. Participating in the project-making process will help teachers understand the directions and be ready to assist pupils with difficult steps. Teachers might also choose to adapt or modify the projects to better suit the needs of an individual child or class. No one knows the levels of achievement pupils will reach better than their teacher.

While it is preferable for pupils to work as independently as possible, there is some flexibility in regards to project materials and tools. They can vary according to what is available. For instance, while standard white glue may be most familiar, there might be times when a teacher will choose to speed up a project by using a hot glue gun to join materials. Where plaster gauze is not available, papier mâché can often be used. Likewise, while a project may call for leather cord, in most instances it is possible to substitute plastic rope or even wool or string. Acrylic paint may be recommended because it adheres better to a material such as felt or plastic, but other types of paint would be suitable as well. Circles can be drawn with a compass, or simply by tracing a cup, roll of tape, or other circular object. Allowing pupils a broad spectrum of creativity and opportunities to problem-solve within the parameters of a given project will encourage their critical thinking skills most fully.

Each project contains a question within the directions. These questions are meant to be thought-provoking and promote discussion while pupils work on the project.

Index

AD and CE 4
alphabet 9
aqueducts 8
army 6, 11

BC and BCE 4

Caesar, Augustus 5, 6
Caesar, Julius 5, 6
census 6
chariot races 12, 15,
    22
children 11, 12, 14
Circus Maximus 15
citizens 4, 11
clothes 13
Colosseum 5, 15
concrete 8, 9
Constantine 5, 7
consuls 4, 6

dice game (activity)
    26–29

education 11, 12
emperors 5, 6, 7, 8,
    12, 15
engineering 8–9
entertainment 14–15
equites 11

families 10, 12
festivals 15
food and meals 12,
    13, 16–17
Forum 14
founding of Rome 4

games and toys 14,
    26–29
gladiators 15
gods and goddesses 4,
    6, 8, 15

homes 10

Justinian Code 8

kings 4

language 9
Latin 9
laws 8
libum (sacrifical cake:
    recipe) 16–17

marriage 12
mosaics 13, 22
mosaics (activity)
    22–25

Odoacer 7

Pantheon 9
patricians 11
plebeians 11
Pompeii 22
provinces 6, 8
public baths 14

religion 6
republic 4, 5, 6
roads 8
Roman Empire 4, 5,
    6, 7
Rome 4, 10
Romulus and Remus
    4

senate 4
slaves 11, 12, 15
social classes 10, 11
sundial 9, 18
sundial (activity)
    18–21

taxes 6
temples 8
Tiber River 4
togas 13

water supplies 8
women and girls 11,
    12, 13, 15
work 11